Solving Problems in Schools

A GUIDE FOR EDUCATORS

*A Practical and Systemic Approach
to Enduring Solutions*

By Paige Leavitt

APQC®

AMERICAN PRODUCTIVITY
& QUALITY CENTER

EDUCATION INITIATIVE

American Productivity & Quality Center
123 North Post Oak Lane, Third Floor
Houston, Texas 77024

Editor
Emma Skogstad

Designer
Connie Choate

Manufactured in the United States of America

ISBN 1-928593-81-x

American Productivity & Quality Center
Web site address: www.apqc.org

Table of Contents

Preface 5

Introduction 9

Chapter 1:
APQC's Problem-Solving Approach 11

Chapter 2:
Define the Problem and Goal 15
  Tool: Data-Collection Plan

Chapter 3:
Analyze Root Causes 21
  Tools: Brainstorming, Fishbone Diagram,
  and Force Field Diagram

Chapter 4:
Generate Potential Solutions and Identify the Best 31
  Tools: Balance Sheet Analysis and Criteria Matrix

Chapter 5:
Plan and Implement a Solution 41
  Tools: Tree Diagram, Task Chart, Implementation Plan,
  and Gantt Chart

Chapter 6:
Monitor the Situation 49
  Tools: Pareto Chart

Chapter 7:
Additional Information 57

Preface

C. Jackson Grayson Jr., D.B.A.
Founder and Chairman,
American Productivity & Quality Center

By now, all educators are aware of the frustrating performance gaps in the educational system. Teachers and administrators have the grueling task of diminishing the disparity between:

- the test scores (particularly in math and science) of American students and their international peers;
- the skill levels of graduating students and the expectations of employers; and
- student performance among socioeconomic classes and among races.

Such gaps hinder the academic growth of our nation's youth, dramatically weaken the quality of available work force for employers, and threaten the United States' ability to compete internationally.

At the American Productivity & Quality Center, we examine the best practices of leading organizations and share those practices to improve organizational effectiveness in business, health care, and government. We believe that many of the tools and knowledge we have gathered can also be applied to improve the American educational system.

The educational system can significantly improve with the right goals, beliefs, and knowledge about best practices that exist, but are not transferred. So I created the Education Initiative to help institutions restructure administrative and academic processes by identifying, adapting, and implementing best practices found in all sectors through benchmarking.

About This Book

As a result of our research and work with schools across the nation, we have created a collection of tools for educators in a number of publications. These guidebooks can enrich the understanding of quality improvement in education and are designed to provide proven, real-world tips, tools, and techniques—on a wide range of subjects—that you can immediately apply in the education workplace and/or on a personal level.

This guidebook takes a common-sense line of attack to problem solving and provides practical examples and organizational tools. An approachable problem-solving process is introduced and explained in a step-by-step fashion for use by teachers and administrators alike. Learn how to systematically solve problems; communicate in a common language; organize relevant information; and collect, display, and use data in problem solving.

Additional Help

APQC is a member-based nonprofit that works with organizations from around the world. A recognized leader in benchmarking, knowledge management, measurement, process improvement, and quality, APQC helps organizations adapt to rapidly changing environments and build new and better ways to work. For the past 25 years, APQC has been identifying best practices, discovering effective methods of improvement, broadly disseminating findings, and connecting individuals with one another and with the knowledge, training, and tools they need to succeed.

In 1997 APQC launched its Education Initiative with a mission to ensure equity and excellence for all students regardless of race, gender, or socioeconomic background. Since then, APQC has worked with hundreds of schools, districts, states, and higher-education institutions to improve student and system performance.

APQC can help your school system to:
- assess student and system performance for improvement and accountability;
- disaggregate student achievement and system performance data;
- analyze data to align standards, curriculum, instruction, and district goals;
- plan and prioritize steps for improvement of instruction and administration;
- transform training and teaching by ensuring curriculum is implemented; and
- sustain continuous improvement in instruction and administration systems by sharing knowledge and best practices.

Learn more about APQC's Education Initiative, including its conferences and training courses, by visiting www.apqc.org/education or calling 800-776-9676 or 713-681-4020.

Wishing you success,

C. Jackson Grayson, Jr.

C. Jackson Grayson, Jr.

Introduction

If you could solve one problem at your school this year, what would it be? Has this problem been addressed before? Do you find that you and your colleagues must address the same handful of problems again and again?

Most prevailing problems within education persist not because of willful disregard, but because processes get off course, underlying theories change, short-range remedies falter, and solutions do not apply to varied classroom environments. As a result, those with the best intentions waste their time and energy until their frustration resurfaces in a new batch of problem solvers who address the same problems and often make the same mistakes.

From dropout rates to teacher turnover to test scores to maintenance issues, this book will tackle how to approach specific problems and find enduring solutions using the appropriate tools.

Problem solving is not continuous improvement, the process of working consistently to improve a situation. Rather, the techniques laid out in this book will help you solve a problem with reckonable boundaries by developing a measurable goal and discovering the best solution to meet the goal. The process introduced in this book can introduce teachers and administrators to a systematic approach for improvement in the course of containing and resolving problems.

Specifically, this book will help educators identify and define problems and their root causes. This guidebook contains straightforward directions to collect accurate data; build consensus; display data for easier analysis; devise effective solutions; make objective, informed decisions; and monitor progress.

Following the logical direction mapped out in these chapters will help both individuals and task forces use their time effectively to ensure problems are fully and systematically addressed. Readers are invited to probe into APQC's problem-solving approach and follow along as a mock-up case study illustrates the usefulness of the corresponding tools at each stage.

Chapter 1

APQC's Problem-Solving Approaches

If successful businesses were to share the golden rule for problem-solving, it would likely be this: Solving problems is best done in a systematic, step-wise process.

For the sake of time and simplicity, many educators have understandably avoided a problem-solving model and instead implemented immediate solutions to difficult problems. Often, though, their results are not those they intended. Although planning may take extra time upfront, skipping the process can be much more complicated, expensive, and time-consuming in the long run. In addition to the original problem, additional problems resulting from a failed resolution may have to be confronted. Furthermore, support for change dramatically decreases with each failed solution. A systematic process, one that involves following specific steps in a certain order, can save time, money, and effort in the long run.

Systematic Approach

In addition to being an efficient organizational tool, a systematic process, such as APQC's problem-solving approach, also enables problem solvers to avoid casting blame and entertaining ineffective solutions. With a well-directed focus and hard facts, systematic thinking will help to;

- organize data (that is, any information collected about a problem);
- untangle unrelated issues;
- sort out symptoms and root causes;
- prioritize critical issues;
- define the problem before leaping into solutions;
- avoid restricted thinking with more creative solutions;
- foster widespread support for the solution;
- plan a realistic solution implementation; and
- monitor data to prevent reoccurrence.

A structured approach to creating an action plan, implementing a solution, and monitoring the situation will ensure an enduring solution.

Proven Methodology and Tools

Far from being a stagnant process, problem solving requires creativity, judgment, and insight. However, flashes of brilliance seldom occur in a vacuum. Systematic analysis stimulates insight. APQC's problem-solving approach adds structure to common sense (Figure 1).

Systematic Approach

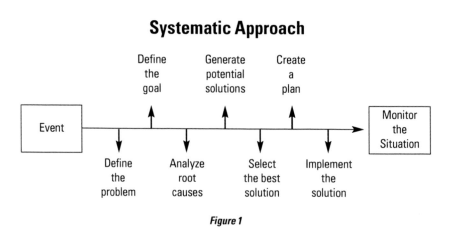

Figure 1

The conventional, step-wise skill process in this guidebook is similar to that used widely in business and government. In this approach, problem-solving task forces use specific tools for idea generation, data collection, consensus building, display and analysis, decision making, planning and implementing actions, tracking variation, and assessing results.

Step by step, this systematic problem-solving approach follows.

1. **Define the problem and goal.** Assess immediate concerns, and if necessary, contain the damage. Then, develop a problem statement, and identify the long-term goal.
2. **Analyze root causes.** Consult experts, review past experiences, use judgment, and conduct a root-cause analysis.

3. **Generate potential solutions and identify the best.** Detail all possible solutions. Assess the pros and cons. Determine the best solutions by defining criteria and using the appropriate tools.

4. **Plan and implement a solution.** Assess the solution's impact on all involved parties, identify obstructing and supporting factors, divide the solution into sequential tasks, develop contingency plans, present the plan to sponsors, and implement.

5. **Monitor the situation.** Anticipate and address problems and reactions, assess the impact of change, and monitor the situation.

This approach provides participants with a systematic but flexible model for use in various situations. One situation might require a close adherence to each step, whereas another problem may not require the same amount of attention. Some steps may need to be revisited if it becomes apparent the process is heading in the wrong direction.

Chapter 2

Define the Problem and Goal

In some cases, educators may need to act quickly to contain the damage. A dangerous situation or pressing parental concerns may need to immediately be addressed, but this is not the time to implement a long-term solution.

First, you will need to develop a clear and simple definition of the problem, as well as a goal for improvement. It is very important for everyone involved to have the same perception of the problem. Otherwise, wasted effort will result in multiple, misdirected solutions.

Define the Problem

Sometimes, the problem is clear and unambiguous from the outset. Other times, there simply exists a vague awareness that something isn't right. The following questions may help to define the problem and its boundaries:

- What is happening, where and when is it happening, and how often is it happening?
- Who is involved?
- To what extent is the situation problematic?
- Are there current processes that are making the problem worse?
- Under what circumstances does the problem occur?
- Is the situation improving, worsening, or steadily progressing?

Although asking such questions helps to establish a group understanding, defining the overall effort is best kept simple. Write down what is understood about the problem. For example, the problem could be that an increasing number of high school students have dropped out, classes are frequently interrupted during instruction, or more teachers than usual have quit this year. To address the direct issue and avoid unrelated problems, the problem statement should then be refined to a few words, using general terms. For instance, the problem may be an "increasing dropout rate," "poor classroom management," or "decreasing teacher retention." Ask yourself:

- Does everyone involved have a common understanding of the problem?
- How can the problem be stated objectively?
- How can multiple interpretations and favoritism be avoided in the wording of the problem?

The problem statement should accurately and clearly describe what the problem solvers want to change, without including blame, causes, or solutions.

Define the Goal

Once the problem has been clearly defined and articulated, the goal should be easy to define. The goal for improvement should also be reduced to a few words. For example, the desired goal for the three aforementioned problems may be to decrease the dropout rate, improve classroom management, or increase teacher retention. Avoid developing goals that do not directly address the stated problem. For example, "becoming the best school in the district" may be your ultimate goal, but it does not directly address the problem of dropout rates.

The next step is to determine the gap between the present situation and the goal. For example, if the problem is that high school dropout rates have risen from .25 percent to 3 percent, then the present situation is 3 percent and the goal is to return to typical rates of .25 percent. The solution must involve reducing the dropout rate 2.75 percent. (If the problem was the occurrence of *any* high school drop outs, the goal would not be to return to typical rates, but to prevent any students from dropping out. In this case, continuous improvement efforts may be your next approach to eliminating any drop-outs.) Having such a well-defined goal allows you to track your progress and evaluate the solution's effectiveness.

Conversely, if your goal is defined too broadly, you may collect inaccurate data, search for inaccurate causes, waste resources, and ultimately, not find a solution. Note that taking on too general of a problem can result in frustrated, confused, or apathetic assistance from others.

Make it a Collaborative Effort

Oftentimes, in an academic environment, problem solving is a group effort. Collaborative efforts should directly involve staff affected by the problem. This can greatly reduce the amount of time dedicated to researching ideas and greatly increase the probability of acceptance of the final solution. In cases where a large group will be affected, members of the group should be given the opportunity to select representatives for involvement.

In a collaborative environment, it is important to ensure that what one problem solver considers general knowledge is considered likewise by the rest of the task force or team. And more importantly, the problem-solving team should come to a consensus on the importance of the issue at hand. Once the problem and goal have been defined, the team should agree that a solution is even needed.

If so, the team should determine how much time can be dedicated to finding a solution. Effective problem solvers proceed by building on and supporting each team member's ideas while showing respect and letting everyone speak. Creating an open, respectful environment prevents the process from derailing through accusations, defensiveness, politics, and personal agendas.

These pitfalls can also be avoided by continuously stressing the need for supporting data. So that every answer is supported by fact, detail:
- what information is needed (e.g., quantities, time, cost, descriptions, locations, and classes),
- where to retrieve it (e.g., databases, reports, time sheets, student records, and test scores),
- how to retrieve it (e.g., visual inspection, interviews, surveys, check sheets, and measurement), and
- who will be responsible for it.

Figure 2, page 18, shows a template plan to collect such supporting data that can be used at any step in the problem-solving approach.

Data-collection Plan

Problem:

Questions	Data needed	Data source	Collection method	Assigned to
What ...				
Where ...				
When ...				
To whom ...				
How often ...				
Extent ...				
Circumstances ...				
Trend ...				

Figure 2

Avoid Causes and Solutions in the Problem Statement

Avoid including causes in the stated problem. For instance, "the dropout rate is increasing as high school students search for full-time jobs" should be revised to "the dropout rate is increasing." Even if elements such as parent involvement, economic issues, student morale, personal conflict, and legislative guidelines are suspected causes, just focus on the problem itself for now. Otherwise, your problem statement could inaccurately infer a specific solution.

(Keep in mind, however, that if a side issue appears to be a significant problem in itself, it may be wise to confront it later or to suggest it be taken up by another problem-solving team.)

Implied solutions should also be avoided. For example, the problem statement, "we need to hire teachers with a greater commitment" should be restated as "teacher retention is decreasing." After all, the solution cannot be assumed without first fully understanding the problem.

Take Data to the Next Stage

To proceed, answer the following questions:
- Were immediate issues addressed?
- Was input sought by those affected by the problem?

- Did the problem solvers reach a consensus on the validity of the problem?
- Can the problem be stated in a few words?
- Is the problem narrow enough in scope to approach?
- Does the stated problem avoid accusations?
- Is the problem stated objectively?
- Were conclusions reached using data?
- Can the goal be stated in a few words?
- Is the immediate containment of damage distinguished from the long-term goal?

Once the problem and goal are clearly defined—without implied solutions or causes—the problem solvers are ready to progress to the next stage. If any additional information is found, the problem may need to be redefined.

Case Study: Moore Elementary

With lower average scores on state end-of-year exams and increasing concern from parents, administrators at Moore Elementary school have organized a task force to address the increasing number of students not passing the exams. The task force, organized and headed by Principal Amanda Genero, consists of Vice Principal Garrett Wrinkle, teachers Victor Freytag and Myra Kennedy, PTA representative Renault Simons, and District Curriculum Coordinator Cleo Mabry.

The task force aims to fully address the issue before the next school year. The task force assesses who should be notified before the nearing summer break; and other teachers, as well as support staff and PTA members, are solicited for contact information over the break in case their input is needed. With twelve more months until the next round of exams, the task force's immediate concern is to start off the next year on the right foot.

Moore Elementary accommodates approximately one hundred students in each grade, although that number is steadily increasing. Academic achievement has varied slightly among classes and from year-to-year, but there were typically only three to four students per grade who did not pass the exam and, consequently, did not proceed to the next grade. In the last three years, however, the average number of students held back per grade has risen from five to seven to eight.

The first step for the task force is to define to problem. Many of the initial problem statements created by the group included implied causes, such as "without adequate educational materials, students are failing exams" and "with increased class sizes, students do not receive enough attention to pass exams." Some of the statements had implied solutions, such as "teachers need more support to help students with academic problems." Finally, the group agreed on the simple problem statement: "More students are failing end-of-year exams." An obvious goal sprung forth from that statement: to reduce the number of students who fail end-of-year exams.

With this focus in mind, the task force needed data to ensure these failures indicated an increasing trend and not a misperception or standard deviation, so they created a data-collection plan (Figure 3). Using average scores from the previous twelve years and taking into account the rising number of students, the task force found that the trend was statistically significant. A discussion of the implications, coupled with already documented parental concerns, confirmed that the problem was of high importance.

Portion of Moore's Data-collection Plan

Problem: More students are failing end-of-year exams.				
Questions	Data needed	Data source	Collection method	Assigned to
What are average scores from the last 12 years?	Test scores	School records	Pull data from existing records.	Genero
At what rate is the student population increasing?	Student pop.	School records	Pull together attendance records by semester. Determine rate of increase.	Wrinkle

Figure 3

Supported by objective information, the task force now proceeded to the next step in the problem-solving approach: to analyze the root cause.

Chapter 3

Analyze Root Causes

P roblems are departures from either a normal or desired state. Deviations show up by comparing what should be to what is. Many deviations result from a change of some kind. Find this change, and you will likely often find the root cause.

To analyze and determine root causes, you must begin by using collected data to determine potential causes. Often, problem solvers, particularly those directly affected by the problem, will have their own opinions about possible causes. Making a conscious decision to thoroughly analyze a number of causes is an important part of the process. By committing to this step, you can find the root cause of a problem without focusing on symptoms of the problem.

As you analyze root causes, be aware that some problems may have more than one root cause. Each root cause will require its own strategy.

Types of Causes

Trace the chain of events that led to the problem. In this chain, a root cause may be compounded by contributing causes that lead to the event. A contributing cause exacerbates a root cause, so it must show a direct link to the root cause, as well as an obvious effect on the problem.

Such chains of events can easily branch off, so be sure to stay within reasonable boundaries and take small steps. Do not focus on solutions yet. Discontinue tracing the chain of events once the problem is beyond your power to fix. For example, if the air conditioning system at an elementary school breaks frequently, the problem might be traced all the way back to limited federal funding or lessening quality in manufacturing worldwide. However, these root causes are obviously beyond the scope of a problem-solving team. A more reasonable cause would be inadequate maintenance on campus. This is a problem that the team can address.

Because there may be more than one root cause, it is important to analyze any potential cause carefully. Potential causes can be classified as common or special. Common causes are inherent in the process leading to a particular outcome. Special causes originate from unusual circumstances that rarely reoccur. For example, an elementary school may typically expect 2 percent to 4 percent of its students to be absent within a week. These absences are commonly caused by family business. If the school experiences an additional 6 percent rise in absences—outside of the typical variation—it may want to search for a special cause, such as an outbreak of a strong cold virus. In many instances, such as the cold virus example, special causes will not significantly contribute to a problem over the long run and therefore will not need to be addressed by a problem-solving task force.

The Process

The process of collecting and considering potential causes is best carried out using collaborative efforts, which follow.

- **Use judgment.** APQC's problem-solving approach should not replace your intuition, but rather assist in confirming or refuting your insights and assumptions. If a cause is immediately suspected, hunches should be heeded and then supported by data and documentation.
- **Review past experiences.** Research if the problem has occurred before (at your school or at another) and how it was resolved, if at all. Patterns are valuable lessons learned.
- **Consult experts.** Process experts such as curriculum-design specialists, payroll vendors, process improvement consultants, service bureaus, and child psychologists can provide an outside perspective and use elevated expertise to solve the problem, sometimes quickly and cheaply. However, be sure to determine that the information experts would provide is not already accessible to the task force. Determine exactly what information is needed, and consider whether or not any previous research efforts have already uncovered this information.

- **Conduct a root-cause analysis.** A probing analysis, conducted by tracing a chain of events, should reveal the root cause. A fishbone diagram, described later in this chapter, is an effective way to organize potential causes.

Seek and Organize Potential Causes

Using feedback from those affected by the problem, list all potential causes. This list can then be narrowed down to the most likely causes. The number of potential causes will likely depend on the complexity of your problem.

These causes can be organized using brainstorming (Figure 4), a fishbone diagram (Figure 5, page 24), and a force field diagram (Figure 6, page 25).

Brainstorming is often the best way to quickly generate a large number of potential causes. The three methods described in Figure 4 are effective. Be sure to avoid criticism, encourage creativity, solicit additional ideas, and try to build on each other's ideas.

Three Methods of Brainstorming

Method	Beneficial Features	Possible Setbacks
Free Wheeling • Randomly call out ideas • Record ideas	• Spontaneous • Creative • Easy to build on	• The strong dominate • Confusion/All talk • Ideas get lost
Round Robin • Share ideas in turn • Record ideas	• No one dominates • Discussion focused • All take part	• Anxious waiting • Loss of energy • Reluctant to pass • Not easy to build
Slip Method • Write ideas on paper individually • Collect and organize	• Anonymous • Large groups • Shy people contribute	• Can't build on ideas • Slow • Difficult to clarify

Figure 4

As suggested in Figure 4, brainstorming does have some setbacks. Without applied direction, the process can be inefficient, and data must still be collected and analyzed. Because brainstorming lacks structure, it is helpful to clarify potential causes that come out of a brainstorming session using a fishbone diagram.

A **fishbone diagram** organizes causes so they can be grouped by categories (Figure 5). To create this diagram, follow these directions.

Fishbone Diagram

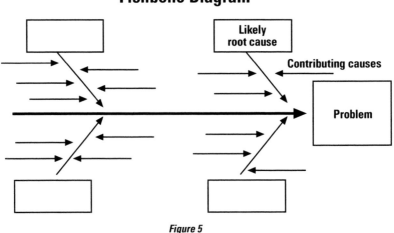

Figure 5

- Construct the form shown in Figure 5. Write the problem in a box on the right side of the paper. The slanted lines represent major categories of causes. Label them using generic categories of causes (for example, people, equipment, materials, methods, policies, and environment).
- Analyze all potential contributing and root causes. Question the cause of each event until you arrive at a root that can be addressed.
- Eliminate any causes not worthy of further analysis. Common sense or available data may dismiss an unlikely cause.
- Acknowledge any cause that is outside your immediate responsibility. External issues, such as poverty in a community,

may be a factor in a problem but will likely not be the issue confronted within this process. Instead, the consequences of those factors must be taken into account.

Force field analysis can be used to determine negative and positive factors related to the problem and goal. This analysis is helpful for confronting factors that may be working against the goal. To create a **force field diagram**, refer to Figure 6 and follow these directions.

- Create a flip chart of a force field diagram, and write the stated problem and goal.
- Determine positive or negative factors that affect the situation. These may involve staff, school culture, educational procedures, students' skills, equipment, or events. Then, divide the factors into those that improve the situation and those that worsen it. The division of these factors (into the right and left columns) will reveal what will contribute to achieving the goal and what may be restraining factors.
- Gather information to verify the positive and negative factors.
- Try to determine why each negative factor is an inhibitor and how, if possible, to eliminate it. Then determine how to benefit from the positive factors. The positive factors may later become potential solutions.

Force Field Diagram

Problem:

Goal:

Positive Factors	Negative Factors

Figure 6

After working with these tools, you should have a good idea of the root cause. Depending on how large and complex the problem is, further analysis may be necessary. This analysis can take the form of measurement, data gathering, interviews, observations of a process, or construction of a flow chart. It could also involve needs assessment, primary or secondary research, benchmarking, or program evaluation.

After you've found the root cause, be sure to revisit your problem statement and your goal statement. Do they still apply? Do they need to be revised in any way? Once you are sure you have a well-defined problem, goal, and root cause, you can proceed to find an effective solution.

Take Causes to the Next Stage

To proceed, answer the following questions:
- Did people closest to the problem provide input?
- Were experts consulted?
- Were past experiences (your own or others') reviewed?
- Did the group heed individual intuition?
- Were root and contributing causes spelled out?
- Were a number of causes selected to further examine?
- Were groups of likely causes organized in a fishbone diagram?
- Will others agree with the selection of most likely causes?
- Were factors working against the goal defined and confronted using force field analysis?
- Were unlikely causes eliminated?
- Were the most probable causes prioritized?
- Was the root cause found and analyzed?
- Do the stated problem and goal still apply?

Case Study: Moore Elementary

The Moore Elementary task force has many ideas about possible causes of the steady rise in exam failure rates. Many of the ideas are related in some manner, so the task force wants to determine a chain of events and identify contributing and root causes.

After an initial brainstorming session, the group members find that their list is disorganized. They also can't be sure that the list of possible causes (see "Moore's Brainstorming List" below) is conclusive. The group members decide to get outside input, so they invite a number of specialists to join the discussion. A curriculum-design consultant is hired to determine if the school's content goals for each grade appropriately parallel state requirements. A representative from the state education agency is asked to describe statewide trends in exam scores, to give a more thorough presentation of recent content changes in the exams, and to provide examples of schools that have been in similar situations. Finally, a member of the city council is asked for input on how the town's population and its demographics are changing. These outside perspectives provide the task force with a more comprehensive outlook and additional objective data.

Moore's Brainstorming List
- Curriculum does not reflect state guidelines.
- Many students are not grasping the necessary content.
- The end-of-year exams are getting tougher.
- Exam content has changed dramatically.
- New students are having difficulty preparing for the test.
- Some teachers are not covering the required material.
- Many students simply aren't capable of passing the exams.
- Students are unprepared for the time constraints and format of the exam.

The curriculum-design consultant confirms that the school's content goals reflect the knowledge needed to pass the exams. The state education agency representative states that few other schools have been experiencing such a downward trend, but offers contact information from schools that have improved their performance and statewide standing. After hearing from these two experts, the task force is more assured that the school has fully understood recent changes to the exam and has integrated those changes into the curriculum. Finally, the city council member describes how the recent increase in the town's population stems primarily from the relocation of the company ABC Inc.'s headquarters. Many of the new residents have been transferred from ABC Inc.'s previous headquarters in another state, and more transfers are expected in the next few years.

This information refutes some of the task force's hunches and reinforces others. Vice Principal Wrinkle had initially thought the problem lay in the curriculum, but he is now willing to consider other potential causes. Freytag, a teacher, thought the problem may lie in particular grades or classrooms, but a breakdown of the test scores shows an evenly distributed passing/failure rate across the school. Some potential causes, such as deeming that some students are simply incapable of passing, are eliminated because historical trends indicate the contrary. The list of potential causes is now narrowed to the following.

CAUSE 1 Most students are not grasping the necessary content.
CAUSE 2 New students are unprepared for the test.
CAUSE 3 Students are unprepared for the time constraints and format of the exam.

Using this information, the group again attempts to find the root cause, using a fishbone diagram (Figure 7). With extended input from the teachers and PTA representative on the task force, the group finds that potential causes one and three (above) may be contributing causes if applied only to new students.

The task force decides that many of the new students are not fully prepared for the exams. A further breakdown of the test scores of students new to the district in the past three years reveals that transfer students who begin the school year at Moore Elementary have a significantly higher success rate on exams than do mid-year student transfers. The task force finally concludes that students who transfer to Moore Elementary after the beginning of the school year are not fully prepared for end-of-year exams. Principal Genero ensures that everyone in the task force has the same understanding of the root-cause statement: "Mid-year transfer students are not fully prepared for end-of-year exams." She then prepares the group to find a solution by creating a force field diagram that outlines the positive and negative factors of the problem and goal (Figure 8).

Detail of Moore's Fishbone Diagram

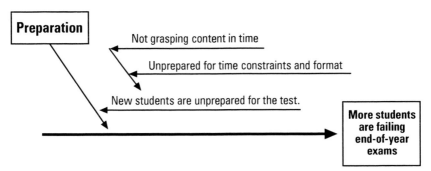

Figure 7

Moore's Force Field Diagram	
Stated Problem: Students who transfer to Moore Elementary after the beginning of the school year are not fully prepared for end-of-year exams.	
Goal: Reduce the number of students who fail the exams to proceed to the next grade.	
Positive Factors	**Negative Factors**
Student capability	Little time to prepare students
Alignment with school's mission	Already overburdened faculty
Parent and teacher support to change existing procedures	Short amount of time to implement changes
Clear understanding of exam requirements	Time spent tutoring transfer students takes time away from covering new material
	Unsure of student's academic skills upon registration

Figure 8

Chapter 4

Generate Potential Solutions and Identify the Best

At this point in the process, you are ready to find a permanent solution to prevent recurrence of the problem. Perhaps you have installed an interim solution while you completed the problem-solving process. The distance between your interim solution and the long-term solution you'll find is the diminished likelihood of recurrence. For example, if staffing is a problem, the immediate solution may be to hire temps and the long-term solution would be to fill the positions. Filling the position obviously prevents recurrences in a way that hiring temps cannot. In another example, leasing temporary space can alleviate overcrowding for a while, but it is a more viable and permanent solution to build or expand in the future.

This section deals with creating corrective actions for enduring solutions, specifically:

- generating solutions (by consulting knowledgeable people and seeking new ideas) and
- selecting the best solution (by narrowing the list to a few choices and then analyzing each possibility).

Generate Solutions

Experienced problem solvers have likely faced a number of roadblocks in their attempts to disentangle educational problems. Bureaucratic issues, such as strict rules and guidelines and tight budgets, can prevent you from seriously considering any solution. But, at this step, it is not constructive to focus on roadblocks. It is time to be creative.

The first inclination for most problem solvers is to consider only a few potential solutions. This is especially tempting under deadline. But it is actually strategically advantageous to begin by generating a long list of solutions, including those that may initially seem unlikely. Simply taking the most apparent solution can send educators into a cycle of continuous damage control without resolution. A more involved idea-generation process highlights innovative and unexpected solutions.

Interviewing, soliciting feedback, and brainstorming may be helpful in this step. Problem solvers should gather input from everyone with a vested interest, including students when applicable. Furthermore, the list of potential solutions can be extended by finding proven solutions to similar problems—inside and outside of your school district.

If you cannot find such situations, it may save time and effort to consult an expert. Many corporations find it cost-effective to pay professional consultants for input about a problem. In addition to having more experience dealing with a particular problem, these consultants will likely lack any emotional attachment to a problem's potential outcome. If outsourcing does not seem appropriate, it may even be helpful to solicit feedback from an expert within the school system who has not yet been involved in the problem-solving project.

Identify Possible Outcomes of Change

As a change agent, be sensitive to the impact that change can have on people. Change often produces negative reactions, which need to be managed. Various factors may obstruct or support a potential solution, and each solution may result in various benefits and drawbacks. To avoid misunderstandings and impractical proposals, list all factors related to each potential solution and then outline potential outcomes or implications. For example, if parents have nowhere on campus to pick up their children, one solution may be to create a driveway next to an already-existing pick-up area for buses. Although parents might support this idea, a shortage of funding could be an obstructing factor. Furthermore, implications concerning traffic flow and the students' safety need to be determined.

To assess the benefits and drawbacks of a potential solution, a balance sheet analysis is helpful (Figure 9). Set up a T-chart, with positives on one side and negatives on the other. List each proposed solution. Through open discussion, analyze pros and cons for that solution. As opinions are aired, a group consensus will usually emerge. From this, the implications can be weighed.

Balance Sheet Analysis	
Proposed solution:	
Positive Factors:	**Negative Factors:**
Proposed solution:	
Positive Factors:	**Negative Factors:**

Figure 9

Select the Best Candidates

Using a balance sheet analysis, the long list of possibilities can be reduced to four to six viable solutions. Integrating similar solutions may also shorten the list. This short list deserves further examination.

To determine which factors and implications should be taken into account, establish a set of criteria (Figure 10, page 34). Criteria might include funding, parental support, student capability, or school board approval. The keys are to select criteria that ensure the problem does not arise again and to consider the primary realistic solutions.

Some criteria may not be as important as other criteria. To accurately compare the criteria in the proceeding criteria matrix, you may want to estimate its' level of importance. This step is a bit more complex, but may highlight the best option out of seemingly similar solutions. Note in Figure 10 that the weighting of the criteria adds up to 100 percent and that each number is divisible by 10. These numbers can then be applied to the criteria matrix (a description follows).

Criteria		
Criteria	**Defined As**	**Weight (optional)**
Control	The extent to which the group can apply the solution themselves	40%
Resources	The extent to which the necessary resources are available to solve the problem	20%
Time	A judgment about the relative length of time it will take to apply the solution	20%
Benefits	The approximate expected payoff from applying the solution	10%
Culture	The degree to which people will embrace the change and the organization can absorb the change	10%

Figure 10

A criteria matrix can help to highlight the best option by structuring measured consideration of all options. First, construct the form shown in Figure 11. List each proposed solution across the top, and list the selection criteria down the far right column. Select a numerical rating system, such as 1= poor, 2 = good, and

3 = excellent. Through open discussion, use each criteria to rate each solution. Work across the form. The highest score by column usually indicates the group's consensus on the best solution, but keep in mind that you are not bound by numbers. A solution that rates slightly lower may still be a viable option.

Criteria Matrix (without weighting)				
Criteria	Solution D	Solution E	Solution F	Solution G
Control	2	1	3	1
Resources	3	2	3	1
Time	1	1	2	2
Benefits	2	3	2	1
Culture	1	1	2	2
Total	9	8	12	7
1 = Poor; 2 = Good; 3 = Excellent				

Figure 11

By weighting the criteria, you can further simplify a complex set of criteria and highlight the best option. In Figure 12, some criteria is listed multiple times because it is more important to the problem-solving team. For instance, "control" weighed 40 percent and is consequently listed in the criteria matrix four times. Each row accounts

Criteria Matrix (with weighting)				
Criteria	Solution D	Solution E	Solution F	Solution G
Control	2	1	3	1
Control	2	1	3	1
Control	2	1	3	1
Control	2	1	3	1
Resources	3	2	3	1
Resources	3	2	3	1
Time	1	1	2	2
Time	1	1	2	2
Benefits	2	3	2	1
Culture	1	1	2	2
Total	19	14	26	13
1 = Poor; 2 = Good; 3 = Excellent				

Figure 12

for 10 percent of the weighted criteria. This disallows less important criteria from receiving equal attention as more critical factors.

With a comprehensive consideration of all potential solutions and an objective set of criteria, problem solvers should now be able to reach a consensus on the best solution. This solution should be both enduring and realistic. The next chapter will show how to prepare to implement the solution.

Take Solutions to the Next Stage

To proceed, answer the following questions:

- Were a large number of potential solutions brainstormed?
- Were people with a vested interest in the outcome involved in generating potential solutions?
- Did a knowledgeable expert contribute potential solutions?
- Were potential solutions imaginative?
- Were similar solutions integrated?
- Were obstructing and supporting factors identified for each solution?
- Was each potential solution evaluated and fully understood?
- Was a best solution agreed on?
- Can the chosen solution be realistically implemented?
- Would the solution, with monitoring, stop the problem from recurring?
- Does everyone involved have the same understanding of the solution?

Case Study: Moore Elementary

To find an enduring solution that will successfully prepare mid-year transfer students for end-of-year exams, the task force must first generate a long list of potential solutions.

The group initially brainstorms ideas. Then surveys are mailed to all Moore Elementary teachers. Teachers Freytag and Kennedy call a handful of their colleagues for a more thorough perspective. PTA representative Simons and district representative Mabry talk to parents who have moved to Moore's district within the last three years. The parents are asked about the transition to academics at Moore Elementary and about what they see as roadblocks.

The task force then reconvenes to analyze the data and extract any additional potential solutions. To compare and contrast each potential solution, the group creates a balance sheet analysis (Figure 13).

The task force uses the balance sheet analysis to anticipate possible results of each potential solution. The balance sheet analysis examines both positive and negative implications. For instance, the potential solution of assigning teacher assistants to work closely with

Portion of Moore's Balance Sheet Analysis

Proposed solution: Assign teacher assistants to tutor mid-year transfer students.

Positive Factors:	Negative Factors:
New students would get one-on-one attention.	Teacher assistants would have less time for other duties.
	Teacher assistants may not have enough time for each new student.
	There is not enough time to properly train assistants for this role.
	Tutoring could be disruptive to the class.

Proposed solution: Put all mid-year transfer students in a special class until they catch up.

Positive Factors:	Negative Factors:
New students would get tutoring they need to catch up.	New students would feel isolated from the other students.
New students could quickly catch up with their peers.	Difficult to identify new students that would not need special tutoring.

Figure 13

new students in class could reduce the failure rate on end-of-year exams. However, the teacher assistants would have to abandon some existing responsibilities and may have trouble providing real-time assistance in the three to four classes they each attend to. Furthermore, their interactions with individual students may disrupt the rest of the class, and time is limited to train the assistants for this responsibility. This is an instance where the balance sheet analysis exposes an unrealistic solution, given the lack of training, resources, and time constraints.

The task force narrows down the list the following potential solutions, each beginning with the same step:

- **SOLUTION A**—Test transfer students upon registration to assess strengths and weaknesses. Teachers would provide new students with private tutoring during study hall. Tutoring would be based on assessment results, and ongoing progress would be monitored until the student catches up.
- **SOLUTION B**—Test transfer students upon registration to assess strengths and weaknesses. Create an extended orientation program that places new students in a small, separate classroom setting, where they each spend one to three weeks adapting to Moore Elementary's testing approach and learning key points already covered in the traditional classroom.
- **SOLUTION C**—Test transfer students upon registration to assess strengths and weaknesses. For each grade, place all new students in a designated class with a smaller size so that the teacher can dedicate more individual attention to problematic subject areas.
- **SOLUTION D**—Test transfer students upon registration to assess strengths and weaknesses. Assign a peer "buddy" to orient the new student to Moore Elementary and to work as a study partner in study hall during the year. A teacher would assess the new student's progress in private conferences twice a month.

To select a solution objectively, the task force creates a set of criteria. Each member has particular concerns. The teachers do not want to add to their already full plate of responsibilities. PTA representative Simons wants new students to feel welcome and be fully integrated into classroom activities. Principal Genero wants a cost-effective investment. And district curriculum coordinator Mabry wants to make sure that new students are enriched beyond exam requirements. These interests are funneled into a generalized list of clearly defined criteria (Figure 14).

Moore's Criteria Defined		
Criteria	**Defined As**	**Weight (optional)**
Effectiveness of solution	Does the solution address the root cause?	40%
Likelihood of acceptance	Will students, faculty, staff, and parents accept the new procedures?	20%
Ease of implementation	Can the solution apply to the next school year?	10%
Durability of solution	Does the solution fully integrate the new students into Moore Elementary?	10%
Cost	Can the existing budget accommodate the solution?	20%

Figure 14

The task force has chosen to assign a weight to the criteria, which was estimated during a group discussion. The task force prefers the solution that will more likely succeed than the solution that is the least expensive.

The four solutions are compared in a criteria matrix, using the task-force's criteria (Figure 15, page 40). The following rating system is used: 1 = Poor, 2 = Good, 3 = Excellent. From this matrix, it is apparent that Solution A, involving aptitude assessment and private tutoring, is favored over the other solutions.

Principal Genero ensures that everyone on the task force has the same understanding of the selection, Solution A. The task force is now prepared to create an action plan and implement the solution.

Moore's Criteria Matrix (with weighting)				
Criteria	Solution A	Solution B	Solution C	Solution D
Effectiveness	3	2	3	1
Effectiveness	3	2	3	1
Effectiveness	3	2	3	1
Effectiveness	3	2	3	1
Acceptance	2	1	1	1
Acceptance	2	1	1	1
Ease	2	1	1	2
Durability	3	1	2	3
Cost	2	2	1	3
Cost	2	2	1	3
Total	25	16	19	17
1 = Poor; 2 = Good; 3 = Excellent				

Figure 15

Chapter 5

Plan and Implement a Solution

In this step, problem solvers must address both the positive and negative effects of the chosen solution. A detailed implementation plan can illustrate how the solution will be carried out and how the effects will be handled. After the plan gains the approval of the solution's sponsors, it can be used to assess progress.

Address Factors

Implementing the solution will bring about change, which often produces negative reactions that need to be managed. Therefore, the problem-solving team needs to:
- understand how the informal organization operates,
- involve people in change that affects them,
- explain the need for change,
- explain the benefits to participants and the organization,
- allow people time to adjust to the change, and
- generate enthusiasm for the change.

In Chapter 4, both negative and positive effects were identified for each potential solution. Now that one solution has been chosen, those anticipated effects need to be addressed.

Identify barriers to change by brainstorming possible negative reactions to the solution. Then, discuss the likelihood that each reaction will occur and the seriousness of each reaction. Finally, discuss what actions could prevent or mitigate these barriers. If possible, the effects of negative reactions need to be reduced. Everyone who will be affected should be informed.

Even positive effects can require planning. For instance, a solution to address a bus route/zoning issue happens to significantly diversify the socioeconomic backgrounds of students at each junior high in a school district. Although the district is happy with this turn of events, it needs to plan how to ease and accommodate the cultural transition at each junior high school.

How each effect will be confronted is then spelled out in the implementation plan.

Detail the Plan

Your implementation plan will be most effective if it preemptively addresses anticipated effects and describes exactly how the solution will be implemented. To illustrate the sequence of steps and the distribution of responsibilities, a tree diagram and a task chart are commonly used.

A **tree diagram** (Figure 16) displays the sequence of steps needed to complete a complex series of tasks, such as mapping the sequence of steps, planning a complex series of activities, or monitoring an implementation plan. Start with the desired goal, and list what must be accomplished to reach that goal. For each task, write what must be done until no further detail is needed. Regardless of where the task is placed in the diagram, an individual needs to be ultimately responsible for each task.

Next, set up a task chart similar to the one shown in Figure 19 on page 47 in the case study. Decide through open discussion how to

Tree Diagram

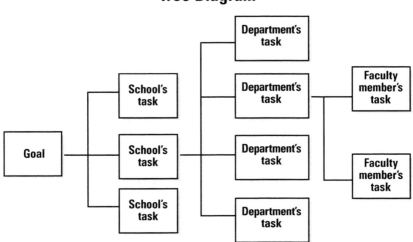

Figure 16

manage all events detailed in the tree diagram. Number each task in the order it needs to be completed, and assign each task. Have each person who has been assigned a task present a list of resources needed, budget required, and a completion timetable. Also determine to whom each person will report.

Make a Contingency Plan

Even in a smoothly progressing process, where each step of the problem-solving process has been fully completed and each organizational tool has been fully utilized, something could still go wrong. When unexpected twists and turns occur, a contingency plan ensures that the entire problem-solving endeavor is not derailed by surprises, delays, or new developments.

Once the implementation plan is finalized, take into consideration what could go awry. Then, plan what will happen if these potential problems occur. By doing this, you may even have the opportunity to prevent surprises and delays in the first place.

Incorporate the contingency plan into the implementation plan. Designate who will be responsible for what and who will decide, as the implementation plan is implemented, if a contingency plan should be enacted.

Report the Plan

The final report should detail the steps for implementation, including the impact on concerned parties and contingency plans. A report outline follows.

A. Problem statement
B. Solution and recommended changes
C. Task(s)
   1. Person responsible
   2. Start date
   3. Estimated hours of commitment
   4. Completion date
   5. Resources needed (e.g., assistance, funds, equipment, and information)
   6. Cost

D. Anticipated implications (including benefits and drawbacks)
E. Anticipated results
F. Contingency plans
G. Summary of what is needed to implement the plan

Once the plan of action is set, present the implementation plan to sponsors (such as the principal or school board) and get approval to proceed.

Implement the Solution

Fully informed and prepared, you are now ready to implement the solution. This step simply involves acting on the wealth of information that has already been uncovered. Follow a **Gantt chart** to keep track of complicated, multiple-task implementation plans (Figure 17).

A Gantt chart illustrates each task's impact on the implementation schedule. Each task is plotted over the time it will take to complete, which indicates what tasks overlap and how other projects will be affected if a task is falling behind.

Gantt Chart: Project Implementation Calendar								
Task	**Assigned to**	**Week beginning**						
		5/1	5/8	5/15	5/22	5/29	6/5
Establish procedure	Powdrell	■						
Train staff in new procedure	Rhine		■	■				
Prepare students	Jones			■	■	■		

Figure 17

Prepare For Evaluation

To proceed, answer the following questions:
- Were both positive and negative effects of the solution anticipated and addressed?
- Were those who will be affected taken into account and notified?
- Was the sequence of steps detailed?
- Were the responsibilities distributed?

- Were needed resources assessed?
- Was an outline for the action plan created?
- Were potential problems during implementation anticipated?
- Was a contingency plan developed?
- Can potential problems be prevented?
- Were findings and recommendations presented to higher levels?
- Did the project receive approval?
- Did all of the problem solvers involved fully understand the implementation plan?
- Were others persuaded that this is the right choice?
- Were negative reactions to change anticipated and addressed?

Case Study: Moore Elementary

The Moore Elementary task force is ready to fully address their chosen solution: test transfer students upon registration to assess strengths and weaknesses and then have teachers offer new students private tutoring based on assessment results and ongoing progress. Tutoring will take place during study hall until each student catches up with the class.

To develop a fully detailed implementation process, the task force must address all factors related to this solution. The group first addresses challenges, such as asking teachers to tutor over their planning period and effectively assessing new students upon registration. How can the administration encourage teachers to give up their planning period? Should the assessment be created internally (over the summer) or adapted from the state education agency's support materials?

The group must also address positive outcomes. For instance, if the tutoring plan is successful for mid-year transfer students, the parents of students who have simply fallen behind will also want private tutoring for their children. Will there be resources available to extend the program to all students?

The task force tries to address these and similar issues in an implementation plan. Initially, the plan has varying levels of details. For instance, the plan draft spells out how to assign and schedule tutoring sessions but does not detail how the school will gain teacher support. To plan such a complex series of actions, the group creates a tree diagram. Figure 18 illustrates a portion of it.

Portion of Moore's Tree Diagram

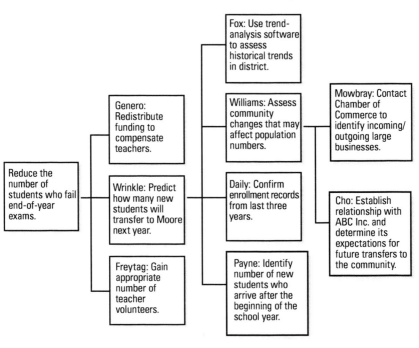

Figure 18

Using all events detailed in the tree diagram, the group coordinates responsibility for the tasks. Because some events must be completed in order for others to be carried out, the tasks are sequenced. Each task force member takes responsibility for ensuring that a particular task is completed, even if the task must be delegated to someone else. The final task chart contains 40 events. (Figure 19 shows a portion Moore's task chart.)

The member responsible for a particular task must research the information needed to complete the chart. Each member must also create contingency plans in case a task falls behind or takes an

Moore's Task Chart					
#	Task	Member Responsible	Resources Needed	Cost	Timetable
6	Predict how many new students will transfer to Moore Elementary next year	Wrinkle	District's trend-analysis software, information from ABC Inc. concerning job transfers	?	May 1 to May 5
7	Estimate average number of tutoring sessions most new students will require to adapt	Kennedy	Teacher and expert consultation, historical data	$400	May 1 to May 5
8	Gain appropriate number of teacher volunteers	Freytag	?	?	May 4 to May 23
9	Redistribute funding to compensate teachers	Genero	School board/teacher union support, aide from district accounting office	≈$20K	May 4 to May 26

Figure 19

unexpected direction. For example, district curriculum coordinator Mabry will be responsible for writing tests to assess new students. The tests will follow the state format to ensure they accurately assess students' abilities to pass end-of-year tests. Mabry creates a contingency plan in case the assessment is problematic. Various reviews are scheduled throughout the next school year to find out if students' actual abilities are consistent with the assessment's initial findings. If not, Mabry is responsible for ensuring that appropriate changes are made to the assessment materials.

Vice principal Wrinkle creates a Gantt chart to monitor activities on the action plan. Figure 20, page 48, shows activities for the first four weeks of May.

Moore's Implementation Calendar (Gantt Chart)

Task	Assigned to	Week			
		May 1–5	May 8–12	May 15–19	May 22–26
Predict how many new students will transfer to Moore Elementary next year	Wrinkle	██			
Estimate average number of tutoring sessions most new students will require to adapt	Kennedy	██			
Gain appropriate number of teacher volunteers	Freytag		██	██	██
Redistribute funding to compensate teachers	Genero		██	██	██

Figure 20

When the task force reassembles, it has the information necessary to fully describe the implementation plan and its contingency plans. A report is prepared for the school board, which approves the change initiative. Because the report is comprehensive and supported by objective data, it is also used successfully to gain support from the PTA and the teacher's union.

With the support of those affected by the solution, Moore Elementary proceeds to implement the solution under the guidance of the task force. With extensive preparation, this step of the problem-solving process is straightforward and easily realized. The task force's new function is to monitor and evaluate progress.

Chapter 6

Monitor the Situation

Often, a problem-solving team or individual can simply run out of energy at some point in the problem-solving process, and the important evaluation phase does not get the attention it deserves. Unfortunately, if progress during implementation is not monitored, the preparation up to this point may well be in vain.

Monitor Implementation

Campus environments are continuously evolving. You can accommodate shifting circumstances and perspectives by tracking implementation and evaluating progress. The person responsible for each activity (as described on the task chart) should monitor implementation and report to the problem-solving team. Key questions to ask are:

- Are we on time?
- Are we on target?
- Are we meeting resistance? If so, why?
- Are we on budget?
- What adjustments are needed? and
- Do we need to activate a contingency plan?

Implementation should be monitored for punctuality, on-target focus, resistance, needed adjustments, budget concordance— essentially whatever determines whether or not tasks are actually bringing the process nearer to the goal. This step may involve creating measures, reviewing each completed task, or collecting data through interviews, observations, and surveys.

Such data may include demographics, enrollment information, graduation rates, teacher evaluations, benchmarking research, and feedback from stakeholders (those with a vested interest in the outcome of the process).

Measures may be used to gauge stakeholder feedback, operational processes, demographics, and student achievement. Stakeholder feedback includes observations, attitudes, satisfaction rates, and values, which can highlight the solution's impact. Operational processes include programs and curriculum or administrative approaches. Demographic measures may include enrollment data or the socioeconomic makeup of the community. (This information can be used to highlight changes in the school's environment.) Finally, student achievement, including grades, test results, teacher observations, and student work, can highlight a solution's effect on the classroom.

If milestones and targets are not met, a contingency plan may need to be enacted. Alternatively, the original task chart may need to be modified to take corrective action.

Assess the Solution's Results

When evaluating progress, the key concern is achieving the desired goal: Has it been reached? Will the problem resurface?

Answering these questions requires data. Plan how to collect this data by determining measures, finding an information source, creating a method to collect data, and determining how research will be displayed. The measures may be performance in critical tasks and finding what lessons learned can apply to the rest of the process.

Finding information sources includes determining how data will be collected, as well as who will collect it and when. For example, when confronting undocumented complaints concerning maintenance issues, a middle school task force designed a template to log and describe each occurrence of a building problem. The administration recorded information on the log. Regular reports were generated based on information from the log. The task force could then review the reports and make the appropriate changes to its maintenance improvement plan.

It may help to gauge stakeholder satisfaction through a survey. Ask whether the situation has improved, what problems have occurred since implementation, and whether the new solution is easy to follow, appreciated by students, useful, and flexible.

A **Pareto chart** may help organize information concerning the relative frequency of specific problems. (Refer to Figure 21 on page 54 in the case study.) A Pareto chart is basically two charts combined into one—one chart is a bar graph indicating the number of each type of occurrence, and the other is a line graph indicating what percentage of the whole that each type of occurrence represents. To create a chart, list implementation issues, such as parent concerns or scheduling difficulties. Then, select a standard measure, such as weekly occurrences. After data have been collected, organize them by category, frequency of occurrence, and percentages.

On the bottom of the chart, list each implementation issue. Arrange the bars in descending order, with the relatively important (taller) bars to the left and the less important (shorter) bars to the right. The left side vertical axis of the chart should be labeled with evenly sequenced numbers to capture the number of occurrences.

The right side vertical axis of the chart should have a percentage scale, from zero to 100 percent. Determine the percentage of each implementation issue by dividing the number of occurrences of each problem by the total number of occurrences. (For example, if there are 20 total occurrences, and five of them are scheduling difficulties, then scheduling difficulties would be 25 percent (five divided by 20) of the total problem.) Plot the percentage line by placing a dot at a height corresponding to the total percentage scale for the first column; as you progress to the right, add the percentage to the previous percentages so that you reach 100 percent in the final column. Complete the line by connecting the dots.

Using the Pareto chart or another display tool, analyze the data. Involved parties should know if:
- the solution is working,
- the implementation plan is on task,
- each task is successful and meaningful,
- procedures are being followed,
- additional help is needed, and
- plans need to be modified.

Standardize Procedures and Monitor the Situation

With such information in hand, you can finally standardize your procedure to ensure that the solution endures. All changes made should be documented. Take-aways from the experience may include updated procedure manuals, revised job descriptions, and new training materials. Furthermore, all involved parties—teachers, students, or supporting staff—should be trained to follow the new procedure. Periodically, especially if the problem resurfaces, you may need to determine whether the procedures are being universally and correctly applied.

Monitoring the situation is not another step in the process, but a final destination that will require vigilance and spelled out responsibilities for the problem solvers responsible for tracking and monitoring the situation.

The Final Checklist

To determine whether further effort is needed, answer the following questions:

- Was progress during implementation monitored?
- Was data collected to analyze progress?
- Were tasks within the implementation plan completed on time?
- Did the data indicate that the solution is working?
- Are stakeholders satisfied with the solution?
- Were procedures standardized?
- Has the desired state been reached? If not, is the problem improving, worsening, or the same?
- Has the solution created any new, unexpected problems?
- Are procedures being followed?
- Do people need more training?
- Could the problem recur?
- What checks and balances are in place to evaluate progress?

Case Study: Moore Elementary

The role of the Moore Elementary task force has now evolved. Rather than simply initiating change, the group now monitors the effectiveness of the implementation plan. This step is critical in ensuring that the group's effort truly results in a decreased failure rate on end-of-year exams.

End-of-year results and state classification will be the ultimate benchmark of the program's success. The group is ensuring the goal will be reached by monitoring each step of the implementation plan. Each member is responsible for particular tasks. The group meets every month to present progress. If a task deviates from its intended outcome so much that it will affect other tasks, the task force member responsible immediately notifies Principal Genero, who keeps the task force and the school board informed of developments.

Because the solution affects a significant number of students and teachers, the task force—particularly teachers Freytag and Kennedy—monitors reaction to the changes throughout the school year. At first, many teachers are upset about the tutoring fee. They argue that although they are paid to tutor, they are not compensated for the time it takes to prepare a lesson plan for a tutoring session. The task force considers this problem but cannot allocate additional funds to the project. Instead, District Curriculum Coordinator Mabry suggests teachers largely rely on the original lesson plans new students have missed and on textbook ancillaries with practice tests included. Furthermore, the administration reshuffles some of its own responsibilities so that teacher assistants can spend less time on administrational tasks and more time helping teachers grade assignments. Consequently, teachers have more time to adapt existing material to tutoring sessions, and the gesture creates an atmosphere of goodwill and of responsiveness on behalf of the administration.

As the solution successfully progresses, initial skeptics warm up to the solution. However, the task force does uncover some concerns through interviews, data sheets, observations, and surveys. From all of these information sources, the task force must determine what problems may actually hinder progress. Vice Principal Wrinkle creates a Pareto chart that tracks the number of incidents of concern (Figure 21, page 54). The chart is reviewed and updated at the monthly meeting.

On the chart, you can see that there were 10 incidents of scheduling difficulties, eight late-year transfers, four observations of underdeveloped lesson plans, four observations of parent concerns,

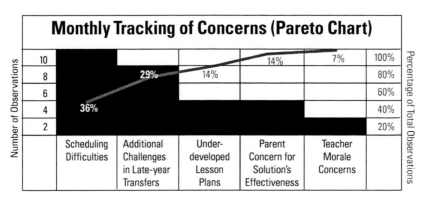

Figure 21

and two teacher morale concerns, for a total of 24 observations. This means that scheduling difficulties made up 36 percent of the total observations (eight out of 24). Using the chart, Wrinkle and the task force can conclude that solving scheduling difficulties should be a primary concern.

To address scheduling difficulties, a new procedure is presented to teachers: When a teacher has more than one student needing to be tutored at a given time, students will no longer be assigned to study hall tutoring sessions with a different teacher. To keep study plans consistent with in-class activities, some teachers will participate in two- or three-on-one tutoring if multiple students are added to the class around the same time. Meanwhile, as procedure dictates, the administration will try to evenly distribute new arrivals to all classes within the appropriate grade level.

Overall feedback indicates that the solution is working, the implementation plan is proceeding as scheduled—thanks to already established contingency plans for small missteps—and procedures are being followed.

At the end of the year, the failure rate for end-of-year exams does decrease. Compared to the year before, the average number of students held back per grade reduces by 50 percent to four, the historical average rate for Moore Elementary. Consequently, the new procedures are standardized through operating guidelines. Parent reaction is positive, and thanks to initial contact with the business

ABC Inc., the school has gained a significant community supporter for future endeavors.

Preventing the recurrence of this problem will involve ensuring that operating guidelines are followed and that test results are consistently monitored. The task force does not anticipate this being a problem. In fact, building on the year's success, the task force now plans to extend the program to all students needing help with end-of-year exams—regardless of whether or not they began the school year at Moore Elementary. The task force knows that its future success lies in diligent attention to the procedures created during the problem-solving process.

Chapter 7

Additional Information

This book has shown a process approach to problem solving. Armed with this experience, educators are ready to launch into continuous improvement efforts. The American Productivity & Quality Center (APQC) can help.

Through its advisory services, publications, training opportunities, conferences, and library of tools and practices, APQC's Education Initiative team can assist you in enabling all students to achieve excellence. Advisory services are available to discover what works, share that information, and connect individuals with the knowledge they need to improve.

APQC also has a number of publications created specifically for educators that are focused on using data-driven instructional tools and strategies to improve student and system performance. Popular titles from APQC's quickly expanding publications catalog include:

- *Closing the Achievement Gap: No Excuses* by Patricia Davenport and Gerald Anderson
- *Benchmarking in Education: Pure & Simple*
- *Benchmarking Best Practices in Accountability Systems in Education*
- *A Framework for Understanding Poverty* by Ruby K. Payne
- *Continuous Improvement Tools in Education: Volume 1*
- *Continuous Improvement Tools in Education: Volume 2*
- *Today's Teaching and Learning: Leveraging Technology*
- *PDCA Instructional Cycle*

These and other titles can be ordered through APQC's online bookstore at www.apqc.org/pubs.

Based on the Education Initiative team's research and experience working with schools, districts, and states, APQC has developed a series of training courses designed to help educators manage and leverage best practices in education. Course titles include:

- ADAPTS Training

- Benchmarking for Educators
- Education Training General Overview
- Knowledge Management for Educators
- Meeting and Facilitation Skills for Educators
- Plan, Do, Check, Act Instructional Cycle
- Problem Solving with Quality Tools for Educators
- Process Mapping for Educators
- Quality Tools for Educators

To find out more about these courses and upcoming conferences—as well as access APQC's wealth of resources—visit www.apqc.org or call 800-776-9676 (713-681-4020 outside the United States).